Table of Contents

Chapter 1: Introduction to Brain-Computer Interface in AI

Understanding Brain-Computer Interface

Brain-Computer Interface (BCI) is a cutting-edge technology that allows for direct communication between the brain and an external device, such as a computer or prosthesis. This technology has the potential to revolutionize various fields, including healthcare, gaming, and education. In this subchapter, we will delve into the intricacies of BCI and explore its wide range of applications.

One of the key components of BCI is neurofeedback, which involves providing real-time feedback to individuals about their brain activity. This feedback can help individuals learn to control their brain waves and improve cognitive functions. Neurofeedback has been used in various settings, such as treating attention deficit hyperactivity disorder (ADHD) and anxiety disorders.

BCI has also found applications in virtual reality (VR), allowing users to interact with virtual environments using only their thoughts. This technology has been used in gaming and entertainment, providing a more immersive and interactive experience for users. Additionally, BCI has been integrated into robotics and prosthetics, enabling individuals with disabilities to control robotic limbs or devices using their brain signals.

In the field of medicine, BCI has shown great promise in diagnosing and treating neurological disorders. By analyzing brain signals, BCI can help doctors detect abnormalities in brain activity and provide targeted treatments. BCI has also been used in cognitive enhancement, helping individuals improve their memory, attention, and problem-solving skills.

Furthermore, BCI has the potential to improve communication and accessibility for individuals with disabilities. By translating brain signals into commands, BCI can help individuals with paralysis communicate with others and control their surroundings. In the field of education, BCI has been used to enhance learning experiences and provide personalized feedback to students.

As BCI technology continues to advance, it is essential to consider ethical and privacy concerns. Issues such as data security, consent, and potential misuse of BCI technology must be addressed to ensure its responsible and ethical use. By understanding the potential of BCI and its various applications, individuals can harness its power for positive impact in diverse fields.

History and Evolution of Brain-Computer Interface Technology

The history and evolution of Brain-Computer Interface (BCI) technology is a fascinating journey that has seen significant advancements over the years. The concept of BCI dates back to the 1970s when researchers first started exploring the possibility of connecting the human brain directly to computers. Early experiments involved invasive procedures, such as implanting electrodes into the brain, to record neural activity. These experiments paved the way for the development of non-invasive BCI technologies that are widely used today.

As technology progressed, so did the capabilities of BCI systems. In the early days, BCI systems were primarily used for basic tasks such as controlling a cursor on a computer screen or typing on a virtual keyboard. However, with advancements in machine learning and artificial intelligence, BCI systems have become more sophisticated and can now be used for a wide range of applications, including neurofeedback, virtual reality, robotics, prosthetics, medical diagnosis and treatment, gaming, cognitive enhancement, communication, accessibility, education, and brain research.

One of the most exciting applications of BCI technology is in the field of neurofeedback, where individuals can learn to control their brain activity in real-time. This can be particularly beneficial for individuals with conditions such as ADHD, anxiety, depression, and PTSD. By using neurofeedback training, individuals can learn to regulate their brainwaves and improve their cognitive function and emotional well-being.

In the realm of virtual reality, BCI technology is revolutionizing the way we interact with digital environments. By using brain signals to control virtual objects and environments, users can immerse themselves in a truly interactive and immersive experience. This has opened up new possibilities for gaming, entertainment, training, and therapy.

Overall, the history and evolution of BCI technology have been marked by groundbreaking discoveries and innovations that have the potential to transform the way we interact with technology and the world around us. As research in this field continues to advance, we can expect to see even more exciting applications and developments in the future.

Applications of Brain-Computer Interface in Artificial Intelligence

In the realm of artificial intelligence, the applications of Brain-Computer Interface (BCI) technology are vast and continually expanding. By harnessing the power of BCI, researchers and developers are able to create innovative solutions that bridge the gap between the human brain and machines. This subchapter will delve into the various applications of BCI in artificial intelligence, shedding light on how this technology is revolutionizing different industries and fields.

One of the key applications of BCI in artificial intelligence is in the realm of neurofeedback. Neurofeedback is a form of biofeedback that uses real-time data from the brain to help individuals learn to regulate their brain activity. By incorporating BCI technology into neurofeedback systems, researchers are able to provide more accurate and personalized feedback to users, leading to improved cognitive performance and overall well-being.

Another exciting application of BCI in artificial intelligence is in the realm of virtual reality (VR). By integrating BCI technology into VR systems, developers are able to create immersive experiences that respond to users' brain signals. This allows for more intuitive and immersive interactions within virtual environments, opening up new possibilities for entertainment, education, and training.

BCI technology is also making waves in the fields of robotics and prosthetics. By enabling direct communication between the brain and external devices, BCI technology is revolutionizing the way we interact with and control machines. This has profound implications for individuals with disabilities, as BCI-powered prosthetics can restore lost motor functions and improve quality of life.

In the realm of medical diagnosis and treatment, BCI technology is proving to be a game-changer. By analyzing brain signals, researchers are able to develop new tools and techniques for diagnosing and treating neurological disorders and injuries. BCI technology is also being used to enhance communication and accessibility for individuals with speech or motor impairments, opening up new possibilities for social inclusion and empowerment.

Overall, the applications of BCI in artificial intelligence are vast and diverse, spanning across various industries and fields. As researchers continue to push the boundaries of this technology, we can expect to see even more groundbreaking innovations that have the potential to transform the way we interact with machines, each other, and the world around us.

Chapter 2: Neurofeedback and Brain-Computer Interface in AI

The Role of Neurofeedback in Brain-Computer Interface

Neurofeedback plays a crucial role in the field of Brain-Computer Interface (BCI) by providing a means for individuals to train their brains to improve cognitive function and control. Neurofeedback, also known as EEG biofeedback, involves monitoring brain activity through sensors placed on the scalp and providing real-time feedback to the user. This feedback can help individuals learn to regulate their brainwaves and improve their mental performance. In the context of BCI, neurofeedback can be used to enhance the accuracy and efficiency of brain-controlled devices, making them more responsive to the user's intentions.

One of the key applications of neurofeedback in BCI is in virtual reality (VR) environments. By using neurofeedback to train users to control their brain activity, researchers and developers can create more immersive and intuitive VR experiences. For example, neurofeedback can be used to help users navigate virtual environments more effectively or to control virtual objects with greater precision. This has the potential to revolutionize the way we interact with virtual worlds, making them more engaging and interactive than ever before.

In the field of robotics and prosthetics, neurofeedback can also play a vital role in improving the control and functionality of brain-controlled devices. By training users to modulate their brain activity through neurofeedback, individuals can achieve greater dexterity and accuracy in controlling robotic limbs or prosthetic devices. This can improve the quality of life for individuals with disabilities, enabling them to perform everyday tasks with greater ease and independence.

Neurofeedback is also being explored in the medical field for diagnostic and therapeutic purposes. By monitoring and analyzing brain activity through neurofeedback, healthcare professionals can gain insights into neurological disorders and develop targeted treatment strategies. Additionally, neurofeedback can be used to help patients improve cognitive function, manage stress and anxiety, and enhance overall brain health. This highlights the potential of neurofeedback in revolutionizing medical diagnosis and treatment through BCI technology.

In conclusion, neurofeedback plays a pivotal role in advancing the capabilities of Brain-Computer Interface technology across a wide range of applications. From enhancing virtual reality experiences to improving control of robotic devices and aiding in medical diagnosis and treatment, neurofeedback offers a powerful tool for training and harnessing the potential of the human brain. As research and development in BCI continue to evolve, the integration of neurofeedback will undoubtedly play a significant role in shaping the future of brain-controlled technologies and their applications in various fields.

Neurofeedback Techniques for AI Applications

Neurofeedback techniques have been gaining traction in the field of artificial intelligence (AI) applications, offering a promising avenue for improving the performance and adaptability of AI systems. Neurofeedback involves monitoring brain activity through sensors and providing real-time feedback to help individuals learn to regulate their brainwaves. By applying these techniques to AI systems, researchers aim to enhance their ability to learn, adapt, and perform tasks more efficiently.

One of the key advantages of using neurofeedback techniques in AI applications is the potential to improve the interpretability of AI systems. By monitoring the brain activity of users interacting with AI systems, researchers can gain insights into how different tasks and stimuli impact neural activity. This information can be used to optimize AI algorithms and improve their performance in real-world scenarios, making them more intuitive and user-friendly.

Neurofeedback techniques can also be used to enhance the adaptability of AI systems by enabling them to dynamically adjust their behavior based on the user's cognitive state. For example, AI systems equipped with neurofeedback capabilities could detect when a user is becoming fatigued or distracted and modify their output accordingly. This could lead to more efficient and personalized interactions with AI systems, ultimately improving user satisfaction and performance.

In the realm of virtual reality applications, neurofeedback techniques can play a crucial role in enhancing the immersive experience for users. By monitoring the user's brain activity in real-time, VR systems can adapt their content and interactions to better align with the user's cognitive state. This could lead to more engaging and realistic virtual experiences, ultimately enhancing the overall user experience and satisfaction.

Overall, the integration of neurofeedback techniques into AI applications holds immense potential for enhancing the performance, adaptability, and user experience of AI systems across a wide range of domains. As researchers continue to explore the possibilities of combining brain-computer interface technologies with AI, we can expect to see significant advancements in fields such as robotics, prosthetics, medical diagnosis, gaming, education, and more. By leveraging the power of neurofeedback, we can unlock new opportunities for creating more intelligent, responsive, and user-centric AI systems.

Combining Neurofeedback with Brain-Computer Interface Technology

Neurofeedback, a form of biofeedback that aims to train individuals to control their brain waves, has shown promising results in enhancing cognitive functions and treating various neurological disorders. When combined with Brain-Computer Interface (BCI) technology, the possibilities for improving brain health and performance are endless. This subchapter will explore the potential benefits and applications of combining neurofeedback with BCI technology.

One of the key advantages of combining neurofeedback with BCI technology is the ability to provide real-time feedback on brain activity. By using sensors to detect brain waves, individuals can receive immediate feedback on their cognitive state and learn to regulate their brain activity more effectively. This can be especially beneficial for individuals with attention disorders, anxiety, or other cognitive impairments.

In the field of virtual reality (VR) applications, the combination of neurofeedback and BCI technology can enhance the immersive experience for users. By monitoring brain activity, VR systems can adapt in real-time to the user's cognitive state, creating a more personalized and engaging experience. This can be particularly useful in therapeutic VR applications for treating phobias, PTSD, and other mental health conditions.

In the realm of robotics and prosthetics, combining neurofeedback with BCI technology can enable individuals to control external devices with their thoughts. By training individuals to modulate their brain waves, they can effectively communicate with and control robotic devices or prosthetic limbs. This technology has the potential to greatly improve the quality of life for individuals with physical disabilities.

In the medical field, neurofeedback combined with BCI technology can be used for diagnostic and treatment purposes. By analyzing patterns in brain activity, healthcare professionals can better understand neurological disorders and develop personalized treatment plans. This technology can also be used for brain-computer interfaces in neurology and brain research, allowing researchers to study brain function and develop new therapies for neurological conditions.

Chapter 3: Brain-Computer Interface and Virtual Reality Applications

Enhancing Virtual Reality Experience with Brain-Computer Interface

Virtual reality (VR) technology has made significant advancements in recent years, allowing users to immerse themselves in realistic and interactive virtual environments. However, one of the limitations of current VR systems is the lack of seamless interaction between the user and the virtual world. This is where brain-computer interface (BCI) technology comes into play, offering a way to enhance the VR experience by allowing users to control and interact with virtual environments using only their brain activity.

BCI technology works by detecting and interpreting brain signals to enable direct communication between the brain and external devices, such as computers or VR headsets. By utilizing BCI technology in VR systems, users can navigate virtual worlds, manipulate objects, and even communicate with others without the need for physical controllers or input devices. This not only enhances the sense of immersion and presence in VR environments but also opens up new possibilities for more intuitive and natural interactions.

Neurofeedback is a specific application of BCI technology that focuses on training individuals to control their brain activity for various purposes, such as improving cognitive function or managing stress. When combined with VR technology, neurofeedback can be used to enhance the immersive experience by allowing users to modulate their brain activity to influence the virtual environment in real-time. For example, users can learn to increase their focus or relaxation levels to trigger specific events or interactions within the VR world, creating a personalized and adaptive experience.

In addition to enhancing the entertainment value of VR experiences, BCI technology can also have practical applications in various fields, such as medicine, robotics, and education. For example, BCI-enabled VR systems can be used for medical diagnosis and treatment by providing therapists with real-time feedback on a patient's brain activity during therapy sessions. In the field of robotics and prosthetics, BCI technology can enable individuals with disabilities to control robotic limbs or devices using their brain signals, enhancing their mobility and independence.

Overall, the integration of BCI technology with VR systems holds great promise for revolutionizing the way we interact with virtual environments and opens up a world of possibilities for various applications. However, as with any emerging technology, there are ethical and privacy concerns that need to be addressed to ensure the responsible and secure use of BCI-enabled VR systems. By exploring the potential of BCI technology in enhancing VR experiences, we can unlock new opportunities for innovation and creativity while also considering the implications for society as a whole.

Virtual Reality Training using Brain-Computer Interface

Virtual reality (VR) has revolutionized the way we experience and interact with digital environments. By combining VR technology with brain-computer interface (BCI) systems, a new world of possibilities has emerged for immersive training experiences. This subchapter will explore the exciting developments in virtual reality training using BCI, and how this innovative approach is shaping the future of education and training.

BCI technology allows users to control digital devices and interfaces using their brain activity. By detecting and interpreting neural signals, BCI systems can enable users to interact with virtual environments in real-time, simply by using their thoughts. When integrated with VR technology, this creates a powerful tool for training and simulation, allowing users to engage in realistic scenarios and experiences that would not be possible with traditional training methods.

One of the key advantages of using BCI in virtual reality training is the ability to provide personalized and adaptive learning experiences. By monitoring the user's brain activity, BCI systems can adjust the difficulty level of training tasks in real-time, ensuring that the user is constantly challenged and engaged. This personalized approach can lead to more effective learning outcomes and improved retention of knowledge and skills.

Virtual reality training using BCI is being increasingly used in a wide range of fields, from medical training to military simulation. In the healthcare sector, surgeons can practice complex procedures in a safe and controlled environment, improving their skills and reducing the risk of errors during real surgeries. In the military, soldiers can train for combat situations in realistic virtual environments, preparing them for the challenges they may face in the field.

As the technology continues to evolve, the possibilities for virtual reality training using BCI are endless. From improving cognitive abilities to enhancing communication skills, BCI-powered VR training has the potential to revolutionize the way we learn and develop new skills. By staying informed and exploring the latest advancements in this field, individuals can gain a deeper understanding of the power of BCI in shaping the future of education and training.

Future Trends in Virtual Reality and Brain-Computer Interface Integration

Virtual reality (VR) and brain-computer interface (BCI) integration have the potential to revolutionize the way we interact with technology in the future. This subchapter will explore the latest trends in this exciting field and discuss how the combination of VR and BCI technology can enhance our daily lives in various applications.

One of the most promising future trends in VR and BCI integration is the development of more immersive and realistic virtual environments. By using BCI technology to directly interface with the user's brain, VR experiences can be personalized and tailored to individual preferences and needs. This could lead to more engaging and interactive virtual worlds that feel truly lifelike.

Another exciting trend is the use of VR and BCI technology in medical diagnosis and treatment. Researchers are exploring how BCI technology can be used to monitor brain activity in real-time and provide valuable insights into neurological conditions such as epilepsy, Alzheimer's, and Parkinson's disease. VR can also be used as a tool for rehabilitation and therapy, helping patients regain motor function and cognitive abilities.

In the field of gaming and entertainment, VR and BCI integration can take immersive experiences to the next level. Imagine being able to control characters in a video game using only your thoughts or emotions, or feeling like you are truly present in a virtual concert or movie. The possibilities for creating new and exciting entertainment experiences are endless with the combination of VR and BCI technology.

For individuals with disabilities, VR and BCI integration offer new opportunities for communication and accessibility. BCI technology can be used to control assistive devices, such as prosthetics or wheelchairs, with the power of the mind. VR can also provide a means for individuals with limited mobility to experience new environments and engage in activities that were previously inaccessible to them.

As we look towards the future of VR and BCI integration, it is important to consider the ethical and privacy concerns that may arise. Issues such as consent, data security, and the potential for misuse of BCI technology must be carefully addressed to ensure that these technologies are used responsibly and ethically. By staying informed and actively participating in the conversation surrounding VR and BCI integration, we can help shape a future where these technologies benefit society as a whole.

Chapter 4: Brain-Computer Interface in Robotics and Prosthetics

Controlling Robots with Brain-Computer Interface

Brain-Computer Interface (BCI) technology has advanced significantly in recent years, allowing for the development of innovative applications in various fields. One exciting area of exploration is the use of BCI to control robots. By harnessing the power of our brain signals, individuals can now interact with robots in a more intuitive and direct manner.

Neurofeedback plays a crucial role in enabling this seamless communication between the brain and robots. Through the use of sensors that detect brain activity, users can send commands to robots simply by thinking about them. This opens up a world of possibilities in terms of remote operation, automation, and enhanced human-machine collaboration.

In the realm of robotics and prosthetics, BCI technology offers new avenues for individuals with physical disabilities to regain mobility and independence. By using their brain signals to control robotic limbs or exoskeletons, users can perform tasks that were once impossible. This has the potential to greatly improve the quality of life for those with mobility impairments.

Furthermore, BCI is being integrated into virtual reality applications to enhance the immersive experience for users. By allowing individuals to control their virtual environment using their thoughts, BCI technology is revolutionizing the way we interact with and experience virtual worlds. This has significant implications for gaming, entertainment, and even education and training.

As with any emerging technology, there are ethical and privacy concerns surrounding the use of BCI in controlling robots. Issues such as data security, consent, and the potential for misuse must be carefully considered and addressed. By staying informed and engaged in the conversation around BCI ethics, we can ensure that this powerful technology is used responsibly and ethically in all applications.

Advancements in Brain-Computer Interface for Prosthetic Limbs

Advancements in Brain-Computer Interface (BCI) technology have paved the way for significant progress in the development of prosthetic limbs. These prosthetic limbs are designed to be controlled directly by the user's brain signals, allowing for more intuitive and precise movements. This technology represents a groundbreaking development in the field of prosthetics, offering greater functionality and independence to individuals with limb loss or limb impairment.

One of the key benefits of using BCI for prosthetic limbs is the ability to restore natural movement patterns. Traditional prosthetics rely on manual controls or sensors that detect muscle contractions, which can be cumbersome and limited in their functionality. With BCI technology, users can control their prosthetic limbs with their thoughts, allowing for more fluid and natural movements that closely mimic the actions of a biological limb.

Another major advancement in BCI for prosthetic limbs is the integration of sensory feedback. By connecting sensors in the prosthetic limb to the user's brain, individuals can receive real-time feedback about the position, pressure, and temperature of the prosthetic limb. This sensory feedback helps users better interact with their environment, improving their overall control and dexterity with the prosthetic limb.

BCI technology has also enabled the development of more personalized and customizable prosthetic limbs. By analyzing the user's brain signals, BCI systems can adapt to the individual's unique neural patterns and preferences, creating a more tailored and user-friendly experience. This personalized approach not only enhances the functionality of the prosthetic limb but also improves the user's overall comfort and satisfaction with the device.

Overall, the advancements in BCI for prosthetic limbs hold great promise for improving the quality of life for individuals with limb loss or limb impairment. By harnessing the power of the brain's signals, users can achieve greater control, functionality, and independence with their prosthetic limbs. As BCI technology continues to evolve, we can expect to see even more innovative applications and improvements in prosthetic limb design, ultimately transforming the field of prosthetics for the better.

Assistive Technologies for Individuals with Disabilities

Assistive technologies play a crucial role in improving the quality of life for individuals with disabilities, allowing them to overcome physical and cognitive limitations. In the realm of Brain-Computer Interface (BCI) technology, assistive devices are specifically designed to help individuals with disabilities interact with their environment and perform everyday tasks more independently.

One of the key applications of assistive technologies for individuals with disabilities is in the field of neurofeedback. Neurofeedback involves using real-time brain activity data to train individuals to regulate their brain waves, which can help improve cognitive functions and reduce symptoms of conditions such as ADHD and anxiety. By utilizing BCI technology, individuals can learn to control their brain activity and achieve better outcomes in their daily lives.

Another important application of assistive technologies in BCI is in the realm of virtual reality (VR) applications. VR technology can provide individuals with disabilities the opportunity to experience immersive environments and engage in activities that may otherwise be challenging or impossible. By integrating BCI technology into VR systems, individuals can control virtual environments using their brain signals, opening up new possibilities for recreation and therapy.

BCI technology has also revolutionized the field of robotics and prosthetics, offering individuals with disabilities the ability to control robotic devices and prosthetic limbs using their brain signals. This advancement has significantly improved the quality of life for individuals with limb loss or mobility impairments, allowing them to perform daily tasks with greater ease and independence.

In conclusion, assistive technologies powered by BCI have the potential to transform the lives of individuals with disabilities by providing them with new ways to interact with their environment and enhance their abilities. From neurofeedback and VR applications to robotics and prosthetics, BCI technology is revolutionizing the field of assistive devices and opening up new possibilities for individuals with disabilities. By exploring the diverse applications of BCI in assistive technologies, we can continue to innovate and improve the lives of those who need it most.

Chapter 5: Brain-Computer Interface for Medical Diagnosis and Treatment

Monitoring Brain Activity for Medical Purposes

Monitoring brain activity for medical purposes is a crucial aspect of utilizing Brain-Computer Interface (BCI) technology in healthcare. By monitoring brain activity, medical professionals can gain valuable insights into a patient's neurological condition, allowing for more accurate diagnoses and personalized treatment plans. This subchapter will explore the various ways in which BCI technology is being used to monitor brain activity for medical purposes, and the potential benefits it offers to both patients and healthcare providers.

One of the primary applications of monitoring brain activity using BCI technology is in the field of neurofeedback. Neurofeedback involves using real-time brain activity data to help patients learn how to control their brainwaves and improve their cognitive function. This can be particularly useful for patients with conditions such as ADHD, anxiety, and depression, as it provides a non-invasive and drug-free way to improve brain function and overall well-being.

Another important application of monitoring brain activity for medical purposes is in the development of BCI-based virtual reality applications. Virtual reality has shown great promise in the treatment of conditions such as PTSD, phobias, and chronic pain. By monitoring brain activity in real-time, virtual reality programs can be customized to each individual's needs, providing a more effective and personalized therapeutic experience.

BCI technology is also being used in the fields of robotics and prosthetics to monitor brain activity and control robotic devices and prosthetic limbs. By monitoring brain signals, individuals with physical disabilities can learn to control robotic devices using their thoughts, allowing for greater independence and improved quality of life.

In addition to diagnosis and treatment, monitoring brain activity using BCI technology has the potential to revolutionize the field of medical research. By analyzing brain activity patterns in patients with neurological disorders, researchers can gain valuable insights into the underlying mechanisms of these conditions, leading to the development of more effective treatments and interventions. Overall, monitoring brain activity for medical purposes using BCI technology holds great promise for improving patient outcomes and advancing our understanding of the human brain.

Brain-Computer Interface in Diagnosing Neurological Disorders

Brain-Computer Interface (BCI) technology has shown great promise in diagnosing and treating neurological disorders. By allowing for direct communication between the brain and external devices, BCI has the potential to revolutionize the field of neurology. In this subchapter, we will explore the role of BCI in diagnosing neurological disorders and the advancements that have been made in this area.

One of the key applications of BCI in neurology is in the diagnosis of conditions such as epilepsy, Parkinson's disease, and stroke. By monitoring brain activity in real-time, BCI systems can detect abnormalities that may indicate the presence of these disorders. This early detection can lead to more timely interventions and improved outcomes for patients.

Neurofeedback is another important use of BCI technology in diagnosing neurological disorders. By providing real-time feedback on brain activity, neurofeedback systems can help patients learn to control their brainwaves and improve their symptoms. This can be particularly beneficial for conditions such as ADHD, anxiety, and depression.

BCI technology is also being used in conjunction with artificial intelligence (AI) to analyze brain activity and identify patterns that may be indicative of neurological disorders. By combining the power of BCI and AI, researchers are able to develop more accurate diagnostic tools and treatment strategies for a wide range of neurological conditions.

In conclusion, BCI technology holds great promise in the field of neurology, particularly in the diagnosis and treatment of neurological disorders. By allowing for direct communication between the brain and external devices, BCI systems are revolutionizing the way we understand and address neurological conditions. As research in this area continues to advance, we can expect to see even more innovative applications of BCI in the diagnosis and treatment of neurological disorders in the years to come.

Therapeutic Applications of Brain-Computer Interface

Brain-Computer Interface (BCI) technology has shown great promise in the field of therapeutic applications, offering new possibilities for individuals with various neurological conditions. One of the most significant therapeutic applications of BCI is in the realm of neurofeedback, where individuals can learn to regulate their brain activity in real-time to improve cognitive function and emotional well-being. This form of therapy has been used to treat conditions such as ADHD, anxiety, depression, and PTSD, with promising results.

In addition to neurofeedback, BCI has also been utilized in virtual reality applications for therapeutic purposes. Virtual reality environments can be created to simulate real-life situations that individuals may find challenging, such as social interactions or phobias. By using BCI to control their virtual environment, individuals can practice coping strategies in a safe and controlled setting, leading to improved outcomes in traditional therapy settings.

BCI technology has also had a significant impact on the fields of robotics and prosthetics, allowing individuals with physical disabilities to control external devices using only their thoughts. This has led to advancements in prosthetic limb technology, giving individuals greater independence and functionality. In robotics, BCI has been used to control robots for tasks such as remote exploration or assistive caregiving, expanding the possibilities for individuals with mobility limitations.

In the medical field, BCI technology has shown promise in the diagnosis and treatment of neurological conditions such as epilepsy, stroke, and brain injuries. By analyzing brain signals, doctors can better understand the underlying mechanisms of these conditions and develop more targeted treatment plans. BCI has also been used in the development of brain-computer interfaces for communication and accessibility, allowing individuals with conditions such as ALS or locked-in syndrome to communicate with others and control their environment.

Overall, the therapeutic applications of BCI technology are vast and continue to evolve as researchers explore new possibilities. From neurofeedback and virtual reality therapy to robotics and prosthetics, BCI offers new avenues for improving the lives of individuals with neurological conditions. As the technology continues to advance, it is important to consider the ethical and privacy concerns associated with BCI, ensuring that individuals' rights and autonomy are protected in the development and use of these technologies.

Chapter 6: Brain-Computer Interface in Gaming and Entertainment

Immersive Gaming Experiences with Brain-Computer Interface

Immersive gaming experiences with brain-computer interface technology offer a new frontier in the world of entertainment. By leveraging the power of artificial intelligence and neural feedback, gamers can now interact with virtual environments using only their thoughts. This subchapter will delve into the exciting possibilities that brain-computer interface brings to the gaming industry and how it is revolutionizing the way we play.

Neurofeedback and brain-computer interface in AI have paved the way for a more intuitive and immersive gaming experience. Players can now control their in-game actions simply by concentrating on specific thoughts or emotions, eliminating the need for traditional controllers or keyboards. This technology opens up a whole new world of possibilities for game developers, allowing them to create games that respond directly to the player's mental state.

Brain-computer interface and virtual reality applications have brought gaming to a whole new level of realism. By combining the power of neural feedback with VR technology, players can now fully immerse themselves in digital worlds like never before. From exploring alien planets to battling dragons, the possibilities are endless when it comes to gaming with brain-computer interface.

In the realm of robotics and prosthetics, brain-computer interface technology is also making waves. Gamers can now control robotic avatars in virtual worlds using only their thoughts, blurring the lines between reality and fantasy. This technology holds immense potential for the future of gaming, offering a glimpse into a world where the boundaries between man and machine are increasingly blurred.

As we continue to push the boundaries of brain-computer interface technology, the possibilities for gaming and entertainment are truly limitless. From immersive virtual reality experiences to controlling robots with our minds, the future of gaming is looking more exciting than ever before. So, for those who want to explore the cutting-edge of gaming technology, brain-computer interface is definitely a field worth diving into.

Brain-Controlled Entertainment Devices

Brain-controlled entertainment devices are a fascinating application of Brain-Computer Interface (BCI) technology that allows users to interact with entertainment systems using only their thoughts. These devices have the potential to revolutionize the way we engage with entertainment, offering a more immersive and intuitive experience for users. By harnessing the power of the brain, these devices can enable users to control video games, virtual reality experiences, and even music and movie playback with their minds.

Neurofeedback is a key component of brain-controlled entertainment devices, as it involves training users to control their brain activity through real-time feedback. This process allows users to learn how to manipulate their brainwaves to achieve desired outcomes, such as moving a character in a game or changing the music track playing in the background. By providing users with instant feedback on their brain activity, neurofeedback helps them develop the skills needed to effectively control entertainment devices using their thoughts.

One of the most exciting applications of brain-controlled entertainment devices is in the realm of virtual reality (VR). By integrating BCI technology into VR systems, users can experience a truly immersive and interactive virtual world that responds to their thoughts and intentions. This level of control and immersion can take the VR experience to new heights, allowing users to feel like they are truly part of the digital environment they are exploring.

In addition to gaming and virtual reality, brain-controlled entertainment devices also have applications in other forms of entertainment, such as music and movies. Users can use their thoughts to control the playback of music tracks, adjust the volume, or even create their own music compositions based on their brain activity. Similarly, users can use brain-controlled devices to control the playback of movies or TV shows, pausing, rewinding, or fast-forwarding with just a thought.

Overall, brain-controlled entertainment devices represent a cutting-edge application of BCI technology that has the potential to revolutionize the way we interact with entertainment. By harnessing the power of the brain, these devices offer a more intuitive and immersive experience for users, whether they are playing video games, exploring virtual reality worlds, or enjoying music and movies. As this technology continues to evolve, we can expect to see even more exciting and innovative applications in the world of entertainment.

The Future of Gaming with Brain-Computer Interface Technology

The future of gaming is rapidly evolving with the integration of Brain-Computer Interface (BCI) technology. This innovative technology allows players to interact with games using their thoughts, emotions, and brain activity, creating a truly immersive gaming experience. With BCI, players can control characters, navigate virtual worlds, and even communicate with other players using nothing but their minds.

One of the most exciting developments in the future of gaming with BCI technology is the potential for more personalized and adaptive gameplay. BCI can monitor players' brain activity in real-time, allowing games to adjust difficulty levels, provide hints or clues, and even create new challenges based on the player's mental state. This level of customization can enhance the overall gaming experience and make each playthrough unique to the individual player.

Another aspect of the future of gaming with BCI technology is the potential for enhanced virtual reality experiences. By integrating BCI with VR technology, players can fully immerse themselves in virtual worlds and interact with them in ways that were previously unimaginable. From controlling avatars with their thoughts to experiencing realistic sensory feedback, the possibilities for gaming with BCI and VR are truly limitless.

BCI technology also holds promise for revolutionizing the way we approach gaming accessibility. For individuals with physical disabilities or limitations, BCI can provide a way to enjoy gaming in ways that were previously inaccessible. Whether it's controlling a character with their thoughts or navigating a virtual environment using brain activity, BCI technology has the potential to make gaming more inclusive and accessible to all players.

As we look towards the future of gaming with BCI technology, it is important to consider the ethical and privacy concerns that may arise. From ensuring data security and privacy protection to addressing potential biases in AI algorithms, there are many important considerations to keep in mind as we continue to explore the possibilities of BCI in gaming. By addressing these concerns proactively and ethically, we can ensure that the future of gaming with BCI technology is both exciting and responsible.

Chapter 7: Brain-Computer Interface for Cognitive Enhancement

Enhancing Cognitive Abilities through Brain-Computer Interface

Enhancing cognitive abilities through brain-computer interface technology is a fascinating topic that has gained significant attention in recent years. By connecting the human brain to a computer system, individuals can potentially improve their cognitive functions and enhance their overall mental capabilities. This subchapter will explore the various ways in which brain-computer interface technology can be used to achieve this goal, providing valuable insights for those interested in maximizing their cognitive potential.

Neurofeedback is one of the key applications of brain-computer interface technology in enhancing cognitive abilities. Through real-time monitoring of brain activity, individuals can receive feedback on their cognitive performance and learn to control their brain waves more effectively. This can lead to improvements in attention, focus, memory, and other cognitive functions, ultimately enhancing overall cognitive abilities.

Another exciting application of brain-computer interface technology in cognitive enhancement is its integration with virtual reality. By combining the immersive experience of virtual reality with real-time brain activity monitoring, individuals can engage in interactive cognitive training exercises that stimulate different areas of the brain. This can help improve cognitive functions such as problem-solving, decision-making, and spatial awareness, leading to enhanced cognitive abilities over time.

Brain-computer interface technology is also revolutionizing the fields of robotics and prosthetics by allowing individuals to control external devices using their thoughts. This has significant implications for enhancing cognitive abilities, as individuals can learn to manipulate objects and perform tasks using only their brain signals. This can help improve cognitive functions such as motor skills, coordination, and spatial reasoning, ultimately enhancing overall cognitive abilities in a practical and tangible way.

In conclusion, brain-computer interface technology holds great promise for enhancing cognitive abilities in a variety of ways. Whether through neurofeedback, virtual reality applications, robotics and prosthetics, or other innovative approaches, individuals can leverage this technology to improve their cognitive functions and reach their full mental potential. By understanding the potential of brain-computer interface technology in cognitive enhancement, individuals can take proactive steps to maximize their cognitive abilities and achieve their goals.

Cognitive Training Programs using Brain-Computer Interface

Cognitive training programs utilizing Brain-Computer Interface (BCI) technology have emerged as a promising avenue for enhancing brain function and cognitive abilities. These programs leverage the power of BCI to provide real-time feedback on brain activity, enabling users to engage in targeted mental exercises that can improve attention, memory, and other cognitive skills. By harnessing the potential of BCI, individuals can tap into their brain's inherent plasticity and drive positive changes in neural pathways associated with learning and cognition.

Neurofeedback, a key component of cognitive training programs using BCI, involves monitoring brain activity through sensors placed on the scalp and providing feedback to the user in the form of visual or auditory cues. This feedback allows individuals to gain insights into their brain patterns and learn how to adjust them to achieve desired cognitive outcomes. Through repeated practice and reinforcement, users can train their brains to function more efficiently and effectively, leading to improvements in various cognitive functions such as focus, memory, and decision-making.

In the realm of virtual reality applications, BCI technology is being integrated to create immersive cognitive training experiences that simulate real-world scenarios and challenges. By combining BCI with virtual reality environments, users can engage in interactive tasks and exercises that require them to focus, problem-solve, and make decisions in a dynamic and engaging setting. These training programs not only enhance cognitive abilities but also offer a fun and engaging way to challenge the brain and promote mental agility.

BCI technology is also making significant strides in the fields of robotics and prosthetics, where it is being used to enable individuals with physical disabilities to control external devices using their brain signals. By connecting the brain directly to robotic limbs or prosthetic devices, individuals can regain lost motor functions and improve their quality of life. These innovations highlight the potential of BCI not only for cognitive enhancement but also for enhancing physical abilities and enabling individuals to interact with the world in new and empowering ways.

Overall, cognitive training programs using BCI hold immense promise for individuals seeking to improve their cognitive abilities, whether for personal growth, rehabilitation, or professional development. By leveraging the power of BCI technology, users can engage in targeted mental exercises, receive real-time feedback on their brain activity, and drive positive changes in neural pathways associated with learning and cognition. As BCI continues to advance and evolve, the possibilities for cognitive enhancement and personal growth are truly limitless.

Ethical Considerations in Cognitive Enhancement Technologies

In the rapidly advancing field of cognitive enhancement technologies, ethical considerations play a crucial role in shaping the future of Brain-Computer Interface (BCI) applications. As we delve deeper into the realm of enhancing human cognitive abilities through technology, it is imperative to address the ethical implications that come with these advancements. This subchapter will explore the ethical considerations surrounding cognitive enhancement technologies and provide insights into how we can navigate these complex issues responsibly.

One of the key ethical considerations in cognitive enhancement technologies is the potential for inequality and discrimination. As BCI technologies become more widespread, there is a risk that only certain individuals or groups will have access to these enhancements, leading to a further divide between the haves and have-nots. It is essential to ensure that cognitive enhancement technologies are accessible to all individuals, regardless of their socio-economic status, in order to prevent exacerbating existing inequalities.

Another ethical concern in cognitive enhancement technologies is the issue of informed consent. As these technologies continue to evolve, it is crucial that individuals are fully informed about the risks and benefits associated with cognitive enhancement before choosing to undergo any procedures. Informed consent ensures that individuals have the autonomy to make decisions about their own cognitive enhancements, without being coerced or manipulated by external forces.

Privacy and data security are also significant ethical considerations in cognitive enhancement technologies. As BCI devices collect and analyze sensitive neural data, there is a risk of this data being misused or exploited for commercial or surveillance purposes. It is essential to establish robust privacy protections and data security measures to safeguard individuals' neural data and ensure that it is used ethically and responsibly.

Furthermore, ethical considerations in cognitive enhancement technologies extend to issues of enhancement addiction and unintended consequences. There is a risk that individuals may become overly reliant on cognitive enhancements, leading to addiction or dependency on these technologies.

Additionally, there may be unforeseen consequences of cognitive enhancements that could have negative impacts on individuals' mental and physical well-being. By addressing these ethical considerations proactively, we can ensure that cognitive enhancement technologies are developed and implemented in a responsible and ethical manner.

Chapter 8: Brain-Computer Interface for Communication and Accessibility

Communication Devices for Individuals with Communication Disorders

Communication devices for individuals with communication disorders play a crucial role in helping them express themselves and interact with the world around them. These devices utilize cutting-edge technology, such as Brain-Computer Interface (BCI), to bridge the gap between the individual's thoughts and their ability to communicate effectively. For people that want to know everything they can about Brain-Computer Interface, understanding the various communication devices available for individuals with communication disorders is essential.

Neurofeedback and Brain-Computer Interface in AI have revolutionized the field of communication devices for individuals with communication disorders. By using neurofeedback techniques, these devices can interpret the brain signals of the individual and translate them into meaningful communication. This technology allows individuals with communication disorders to express themselves in ways that were previously impossible, giving them a new sense of independence and empowerment.

Brain-Computer Interface and Virtual Reality Applications have also shown great promise in the development of communication devices for individuals with communication disorders. Virtual reality environments can provide a safe and controlled space for individuals to practice their communication skills, allowing them to build confidence and improve their abilities over time. By combining BCI technology with virtual reality, these communication devices can offer a truly immersive and effective communication experience for individuals with communication disorders.

In addition to virtual reality, Brain-Computer Interface in Robotics and Prosthetics has opened up new possibilities for communication devices for individuals with communication disorders. By integrating BCI technology with robotic devices or prosthetics, individuals can use their thoughts to control these devices and communicate with others in a more natural and intuitive way. This innovative approach to communication devices has the potential to revolutionize the lives of individuals with communication disorders, giving them greater independence and freedom in their daily lives.

Overall, communication devices for individuals with communication disorders are continuously evolving and improving thanks to advancements in Brain-Computer Interface technology. These devices offer a lifeline to individuals who may struggle to communicate through traditional means, giving them a voice and a way to connect with the world around them. As technology continues to advance, the possibilities for communication devices for individuals with communication disorders are endless, offering hope and support to those in need.

Brain-Computer Interface for Augmentative and Alternative Communication

Brain-Computer Interface (BCI) technology has revolutionized the field of Augmentative and Alternative Communication (AAC) by providing individuals with severe physical disabilities a means to communicate effectively. By using BCI systems, individuals can control communication devices such as speech-generating devices, computers, and smartphones using only their brain activity. This technology has opened up new possibilities for those who are unable to communicate through traditional means, giving them a voice and independence they may not have had before.

One of the key benefits of using BCI for AAC is its ability to bypass the need for physical input, making it ideal for individuals with conditions such as locked-in syndrome, ALS, or severe cerebral palsy. By simply using their brain signals to select letters, words, or phrases on a screen, users can generate speech or text output in real-time. This not only enhances their communication abilities but also improves their quality of life by giving them more control over their environment and interactions with others.

Neurofeedback is an essential component of BCI for AAC, as it involves training individuals to modulate their brain activity to control communication devices effectively. Through repeated practice and feedback, users can learn to generate specific brain signals that correspond to different commands or actions on the device. This process helps improve the accuracy and speed of communication, allowing users to express themselves more fluently and efficiently.

BCI technology has also been integrated into virtual reality applications to enhance the communication experience for individuals with disabilities. By immersing users in virtual environments, BCI systems can provide a more engaging and interactive platform for communication training and practice. This not only makes the learning process more enjoyable but also helps users develop their communication skills more effectively in a realistic and stimulating setting.

Overall, BCI for AAC holds great potential for improving the lives of individuals with severe communication disabilities. By harnessing the power of brain signals, this technology offers a unique and innovative solution for enhancing communication and accessibility for those who need it most. As research and development in this field continue to advance, we can expect to see even more exciting applications and benefits of BCI for AAC in the future.

Improving Accessibility for Individuals with Disabilities

Improving accessibility for individuals with disabilities is a crucial aspect of Brain-Computer Interface (BCI) technology. BCI has the potential to empower individuals with physical disabilities by providing them with alternative means of communication and control. By utilizing BCI technology, individuals with disabilities can interact with computers and other devices using only their brain signals, bypassing the need for traditional input methods such as keyboards or joysticks.

Neurofeedback and BCI in AI play a significant role in improving accessibility for individuals with disabilities. Neurofeedback training can help individuals learn how to control their brain signals more effectively, which is essential for successful BCI operation. By incorporating neurofeedback techniques into BCI systems, individuals with disabilities can improve their ability to communicate and interact with the world around them.

BCI technology is also being used in virtual reality applications to enhance accessibility for individuals with disabilities. Virtual reality environments can provide a safe and immersive space for individuals to practice using BCI technology without the limitations of the physical world. By integrating BCI into virtual reality applications, individuals with disabilities can experience new forms of communication and interaction that were previously inaccessible to them.

In the field of robotics and prosthetics, BCI technology is revolutionizing the way individuals with disabilities can control artificial limbs and devices. By using BCI technology to directly link the brain to robotic prosthetics, individuals can regain lost motor functions and improve their overall quality of life. This level of control and precision would not be possible without the advancements in BCI technology, making it a valuable tool for improving accessibility for individuals with disabilities.

Overall, BCI technology has the potential to greatly enhance accessibility for individuals with disabilities across a wide range of applications. Whether it be in medical diagnosis and treatment, gaming and entertainment, cognitive enhancement, communication, or education, BCI technology can provide individuals with disabilities with new opportunities for independence and empowerment. It is essential that we continue to explore and develop BCI technology to improve accessibility for all individuals, regardless of their abilities.

Chapter 9: Brain-Computer Interface in Education and Training

Enhancing Learning Experiences with Brain-Computer Interface

Enhancing learning experiences with brain-computer interface technology is a fascinating area of study that holds great promise for revolutionizing education. By combining the power of artificial intelligence with neurofeedback, educators can create personalized learning experiences tailored to each student's unique needs and abilities. This comprehensive guide will explore the various applications of brain-computer interface in AI and how they can be harnessed to enhance the learning process.

Neurofeedback, a technique that allows individuals to control their brain activity through real-time feedback, is a key component of brain-computer interface technology. By using neurofeedback, students can learn to focus their attention, regulate their emotions, and improve their cognitive abilities. This can lead to improved academic performance, increased engagement, and a deeper understanding of complex concepts.

In addition to neurofeedback, brain-computer interface technology can also be integrated into virtual reality applications to create immersive learning experiences. By using brain signals to control virtual environments, students can engage with course material in a whole new way, making learning more interactive and engaging. This has the potential to revolutionize the way we think about education and make learning more accessible and enjoyable for all students.

Brain-computer interface technology is not limited to virtual reality applications – it also has practical applications in robotics and prosthetics. By using brain signals to control robotic devices or prosthetic limbs, individuals with disabilities can regain mobility and independence. This technology has the potential to transform the lives of people with physical disabilities and open up new possibilities for learning and exploration.

In conclusion, brain-computer interface technology has the potential to enhance learning experiences in a variety of ways. From personalized neurofeedback training to immersive virtual reality applications, this technology has the power to revolutionize education and make learning more accessible and engaging for all students. By exploring the various applications of brain-computer interface in AI, educators can unlock new possibilities for teaching and learning that were once thought impossible.

Training Simulations using Brain-Computer Interface Technology

Training simulations using Brain-Computer Interface (BCI) technology have revolutionized the way individuals learn and practice various skills. By utilizing BCI technology, users are able to control and interact with virtual environments using only their brain signals, making training simulations more immersive and effective. This subchapter will explore the applications of BCI technology in training simulations and how it is shaping the future of education and skill development.

One of the key benefits of using BCI technology in training simulations is the ability to provide real-time feedback to users based on their brain activity. This feedback can help users understand their cognitive processes and make adjustments to improve their performance. For example, in a flight simulator, pilots can train their cognitive abilities and decision-making skills by receiving feedback on their brain activity patterns during different scenarios.

Furthermore, BCI technology allows for personalized training experiences based on individual brain signals. By analyzing brain activity, training simulations can adapt to the user's cognitive abilities and learning preferences, providing a customized learning experience. This personalized approach can lead to faster skill acquisition and better retention of knowledge compared to traditional training methods.

In addition to individualized training, BCI technology also enables collaborative training simulations where multiple users can interact and cooperate in a virtual environment. This type of training is particularly beneficial for team-based activities, such as military operations or emergency response scenarios, where communication and coordination are essential. By using BCI technology, teams can improve their decision-making skills and enhance their ability to work together effectively.

Overall, training simulations using BCI technology offer a new and innovative way to enhance learning and skill development across various domains. Whether it is in education, healthcare, or professional training, BCI technology has the potential to revolutionize the way we acquire and master new skills. As the field of BCI continues to advance, we can expect to see even more sophisticated training simulations that push the boundaries of what is possible with brain-computer interfaces.

The Future of Education with Brain-Computer Interface Integration

The future of education is rapidly evolving with the integration of Brain-Computer Interface (BCI) technology. BCI allows for direct communication between the brain and external devices, opening up a world of possibilities in the field of education. By harnessing the power of BCI, educators can better understand how students learn and tailor their teaching methods to individual needs.

Neurofeedback is one application of BCI that shows great promise in education. By monitoring brain activity in real-time, neurofeedback can help students improve their focus, attention, and cognitive abilities. This technology has the potential to revolutionize the way we teach and learn, making education more personalized and effective.

BCI integration in virtual reality (VR) applications is another exciting development in education. By immersing students in virtual environments, educators can create engaging and interactive learning experiences that cater to different learning styles. This technology has the potential to make education more accessible and engaging for all students, regardless of their backgrounds or abilities.

In addition to VR applications, BCI technology is also being used in robotics and prosthetics to assist individuals with physical disabilities. By connecting the brain directly to external devices, BCI can help students with disabilities participate more fully in the educational experience. This technology has the potential to level the playing field for all students, allowing them to reach their full potential.

Overall, the integration of BCI technology in education holds great promise for the future. By harnessing the power of the brain, educators can create more personalized, immersive, and engaging learning experiences for students. As we continue to explore the possibilities of BCI in education, it is important to consider the ethical and privacy concerns that come with this technology. By addressing these issues proactively, we can ensure that BCI technology is used responsibly and ethically in the field of education.

Chapter 10: Brain-Computer Interface in Neurology and Brain Research

Studying Brain Function with Brain-Computer Interface

Studying brain function with brain-computer interface (BCI) technology has revolutionized the way we understand and interact with the human brain.

BCI allows for direct communication between the brain and external devices, opening up a world of possibilities for research and application. In this subchapter, we will explore the various ways in which BCI is being used to study brain function and advance our knowledge of the brain.

One of the most exciting applications of BCI in brain research is neurofeedback. Neurofeedback is a technique that uses real-time brain activity data to help individuals learn to regulate their brain function. With BCI technology, researchers can provide instant feedback on brain activity, allowing individuals to train their brains to improve cognitive function, emotional regulation, and overall well-being. This has profound implications for the treatment of neurological and psychiatric disorders, as well as for cognitive enhancement and performance optimization.

BCI technology is also being used in virtual reality (VR) applications to study brain function. By combining BCI with VR technology, researchers can create immersive environments that allow for precise control and monitoring of brain activity. This enables researchers to study how the brain responds to different stimuli and situations in a highly controlled and realistic setting. VR-BCI systems are being used to study everything from cognitive processes to emotional responses, offering new insights into how the brain functions in various contexts.

In the field of robotics and prosthetics, BCI is being used to develop advanced systems that can be controlled directly by the brain. By connecting the brain to external devices, individuals with disabilities can regain control over their movements and interact with the world in new ways. BCI-controlled prosthetic limbs, for example, are allowing amputees to regain dexterity and mobility, while BCI-controlled robotic systems are enabling new forms of human-machine interaction. These advancements are not only improving the quality of life for individuals with disabilities but also pushing the boundaries of what is possible in human-robot collaboration.

Overall, BCI technology is revolutionizing the way we study brain function and interact with the brain. From neurofeedback and VR applications to robotics and prosthetics, BCI is opening up new avenues for research and application in a wide range of fields. As we continue to explore the potential of BCI, we are sure to uncover new insights into the workings of the brain and develop innovative solutions for a variety of challenges.

Whether you are interested in cognitive enhancement, medical diagnosis, gaming, or communication, BCI has something to offer for everyone.

Advancements in Brain-Computer Interface for Neuroscience Research

Advancements in brain-computer interface (BCI) technology have revolutionized neuroscience research in recent years. This subchapter will delve into the latest developments in BCI for neuroscience research, providing a comprehensive overview for those eager to explore the intersection of technology and the human brain.

Neurofeedback, a technique that uses real-time feedback to train individuals to control their brain activity, has seen significant advancements with the integration of BCI technology. Researchers are now able to monitor and manipulate brain signals more accurately, allowing for targeted interventions in neurological disorders and cognitive enhancement. This synergy between neurofeedback and BCI holds great promise for enhancing our understanding of the brain and developing personalized treatment approaches.

Virtual reality (VR) applications of BCI have also seen remarkable progress, enabling users to interact with virtual environments using only their brain signals. This technology has vast implications for rehabilitation, education, and entertainment, offering immersive experiences that can enhance learning and cognitive skills. The integration of BCI with VR has opened up new avenues for research in neurology, psychology, and human-computer interaction.

BCI technology has also made significant strides in the fields of robotics and prosthetics, allowing individuals with physical disabilities to control external devices using their brain signals. This has revolutionized the field of assistive technology, providing greater independence and mobility to individuals with motor impairments. The development of brain-controlled prosthetic limbs and exoskeletons showcases the potential of BCI in enhancing the quality of life for individuals with disabilities.

In the realm of medical diagnosis and treatment, BCI technology has shown promise in revolutionizing healthcare practices. From detecting early signs of neurological disorders to enabling brain-computer interfaces for communication in patients with locked-in syndrome, BCI has the potential to transform the way we approach neurological conditions. The integration of BCI with medical devices and imaging techniques holds the key to personalized and precise healthcare interventions, paving the way for a new era of neurology and brain research.

Clinical Applications of Brain-Computer Interface in Neurology

Clinical applications of Brain-Computer Interface (BCI) in neurology have shown promising results in the field of diagnosing and treating various neurological disorders. BCI technology allows for direct communication between the brain and external devices, opening up new possibilities for understanding and manipulating brain activity. In this subchapter, we will explore the different ways in which BCI is being used in neurology to improve patient care and advance our understanding of the brain.

One of the key applications of BCI in neurology is in the diagnosis and treatment of conditions such as epilepsy and Parkinson's disease. BCI technology can be used to monitor brain activity in real-time, allowing for more accurate and timely diagnosis of these conditions. Additionally, BCI devices can be used to deliver targeted stimulation to specific areas of the brain, helping to alleviate symptoms and improve patient outcomes.

Another important application of BCI in neurology is in the field of neurorehabilitation. BCI technology can be used to help patients recover lost motor function after a stroke or spinal cord injury. By allowing patients to control external devices using their brain signals, BCI can help to retrain the brain and improve motor function in a way that traditional therapies cannot.

BCI technology is also being used in neurology research to better understand the mechanisms underlying various neurological disorders. By studying brain activity in real-time using BCI, researchers can gain valuable insights into how the brain functions and how it is affected by different conditions. This knowledge can then be used to develop new treatments and therapies for neurological disorders.

Overall, the clinical applications of BCI in neurology are vast and varied, offering new possibilities for diagnosing, treating, and understanding neurological conditions. As this technology continues to advance, we can expect to see even more innovative applications of BCI in the field of neurology, ultimately leading to improved patient care and outcomes.

Chapter 11: Brain-Computer Interface Ethics and Privacy Concerns

Ethical Considerations in Brain-Computer Interface Development

In the development of Brain-Computer Interface (BCI) technology, ethical considerations play a crucial role in ensuring the responsible and safe use of this innovative technology. As we delve into the realm of BCI development, it is essential to consider the ethical implications that arise from the intersection of neuroscience, artificial intelligence, and human-computer interaction. This subchapter will explore some of the key ethical considerations in BCI development and how they impact the field.

One of the primary ethical considerations in BCI development is the issue of consent and autonomy. As BCI technology allows for direct communication between the brain and computer systems, questions arise about who has the right to access and control this information. It is essential to ensure that individuals using BCIs have full control over their data and are informed about how it will be used. Additionally, obtaining informed consent from users is crucial to ensure that they understand the potential risks and benefits of using BCI technology.

Another important ethical consideration in BCI development is the issue of privacy and data security. As BCIs collect sensitive neural data from users, there is a risk of this information being misused or accessed without consent. Developers must implement robust security measures to protect user data and ensure that it is not vulnerable to hacking or unauthorized access. Additionally, it is important to establish clear guidelines on how this data will be used and shared to protect user privacy.

BCI technology also raises ethical questions about its potential impact on society and individuals. As BCIs become more advanced and widespread, there is a concern about how they may affect social dynamics, personal identity, and even human rights. It is crucial for developers to consider these implications and work towards creating BCIs that enhance human capabilities without compromising ethical values. This requires ongoing dialogue and collaboration between researchers, policymakers, and ethicists to ensure that BCI technology is developed and used responsibly.

In conclusion, ethical considerations are a critical aspect of BCI development that must be carefully addressed to ensure the responsible and ethical use of this technology. By considering issues such as consent, privacy, and societal impact, developers can work towards creating BCIs that benefit society while upholding ethical principles. As we continue to explore the potential applications of BCI technology, it is essential to prioritize ethical considerations to ensure that this technology is used ethically and responsibly.

Privacy Issues in Brain-Computer Interface Technologies

Privacy is a critical concern when it comes to brain-computer interface (BCI) technologies. These revolutionary technologies have the potential to greatly enhance our lives, but they also raise significant privacy issues that must be addressed. As we continue to integrate BCIs into various applications, it is essential to understand the potential privacy risks and take steps to mitigate them.

One of the primary privacy concerns with BCI technologies is the collection and storage of sensitive brain data. BCIs are designed to read and interpret brain signals, which can provide valuable insights into a person's thoughts, emotions, and intentions. This data is highly personal and should be treated with the utmost care to prevent unauthorized access or misuse.

Another privacy issue with BCIs is the potential for data breaches. As with any technology that relies on data storage and transmission, there is always a risk of hackers gaining access to sensitive information. In the case of BCIs, a data breach could have serious consequences, ranging from identity theft to the manipulation of a person's thoughts or actions.

Furthermore, there is the concern of consent and control over personal data in the context of BCIs. Users must have the ability to control what data is collected, how it is used, and who has access to it. Without proper safeguards in place, there is a risk that individuals could be unknowingly subjected to invasive data collection practices or have their private thoughts and feelings exposed without their consent.

In conclusion, privacy issues in BCI technologies are complex and multifaceted, requiring careful consideration and proactive measures to protect individuals' sensitive data. As we continue to explore the potential applications of BCIs in various fields, it is crucial to prioritize privacy and security to ensure that these technologies are used ethically and responsibly. By addressing these privacy concerns head-on, we can harness the full potential of BCIs while safeguarding the rights and autonomy of individuals.

Regulatory Frameworks for Ensuring Ethical Use of Brain-Computer Interface

In the rapidly evolving field of Brain-Computer Interface (BCI) technology, it is crucial to establish regulatory frameworks that ensure the ethical use of such powerful tools. These frameworks are essential to protect the privacy and autonomy of individuals using BCIs, as well as to prevent misuse or abuse of this technology. In this subchapter, we will explore the various regulatory mechanisms that have been proposed or implemented to govern the ethical use of BCIs in different applications.

One key aspect of regulatory frameworks for BCIs is the need for clear guidelines on informed consent. Informed consent is essential to ensure that individuals fully understand the risks and benefits of using BCIs, and are able to make an informed decision about whether to participate in BCI-related activities. Regulatory bodies and research institutions must establish protocols for obtaining informed consent from participants, taking into account the unique challenges posed by BCIs, such as the potential for invasive or non-invasive brain monitoring.

Another important consideration in the regulation of BCIs is the protection of privacy and data security. BCIs often involve the collection and analysis of sensitive neural data, which raises concerns about the potential for unauthorized access or misuse of this information. Regulatory frameworks must include provisions for data encryption, anonymization, and secure storage to protect the privacy of BCI users and prevent unauthorized access to their neural data.

In addition to privacy concerns, regulatory frameworks for BCIs must also address issues of equity and accessibility. It is important to ensure that BCIs are accessible to individuals from diverse backgrounds and with different abilities, and that they do not perpetuate existing inequalities or discrimination. Regulatory bodies should work to promote equal access to BCI technology, and to ensure that it is used in a way that benefits all members of society.

Finally, regulatory frameworks for BCIs should include mechanisms for monitoring and enforcing compliance with ethical guidelines. This may involve the establishment of oversight committees, ethical review boards, or other regulatory bodies to review and approve BCI research protocols, ensure adherence to ethical standards, and investigate any reported violations. By implementing robust regulatory frameworks, we can help to ensure that BCIs are used ethically and responsibly in a wide range of applications, from healthcare to entertainment and beyond.

Conclusion

In conclusion, the field of Brain-Computer Interface (BCI) in AI is rapidly expanding and offering a wide range of applications that have the potential to revolutionize various industries. This comprehensive guide has covered all aspects of BCI in AI, from neurofeedback to virtual reality applications, robotics and prosthetics, medical diagnosis and treatment, gaming and entertainment, cognitive enhancement, communication and accessibility, education and training, neurology and brain research, as well as the ethical and privacy concerns surrounding this technology.

Neurofeedback and BCI in AI have shown promising results in improving cognitive functions, managing stress, and enhancing overall well-being. By using real-time feedback from the brain, individuals can learn to self-regulate their brain activity and achieve optimal performance in various tasks.

The integration of BCI in virtual reality applications has opened up new possibilities for immersive experiences and interactive simulations. From gaming to therapy, virtual reality combined with BCI technology has the potential to enhance learning, rehabilitation, and entertainment experiences.

BCI in robotics and prosthetics is leading to the development of advanced prosthetic limbs and robotic devices that can be controlled directly by the user's brain signals. This technology is improving the quality of life for individuals with physical disabilities by restoring their ability to perform everyday tasks with greater independence and precision.

In the field of medical diagnosis and treatment, BCI technology is enabling healthcare professionals to monitor brain activity, diagnose neurological disorders, and develop personalized treatment plans. This innovative approach is revolutionizing the healthcare industry and improving patient outcomes through early detection and targeted interventions. Overall, the potential of BCI in AI is limitless, and its impact on society is just beginning to unfold. As this technology continues to evolve, it is essential to address ethical and privacy concerns to ensure that BCI applications are developed and used responsibly for the benefit of humanity.

Future Trends and Implications of Brain-Computer Interface in AI

As we look towards the future of Brain-Computer Interface (BCI) in Artificial Intelligence (AI), there are several emerging trends and implications that are shaping the landscape of this technology. One of the key trends that we are seeing is the integration of BCI with AI algorithms to enhance cognitive capabilities and improve user experience. This fusion of BCI and AI has the potential to revolutionize various industries, from healthcare to entertainment, by enabling more immersive and personalized experiences for users.

Neurofeedback, a technique that uses real-time monitoring of brain activity to provide feedback to the user, is also gaining traction in the field of BCI in AI. By leveraging neurofeedback, BCI systems can adapt and learn from the user's brain signals, leading to more efficient and effective interactions. This approach is particularly promising for applications such as mental health treatment, where personalized feedback can help individuals manage conditions like anxiety and depression.

Another exciting trend in BCI in AI is the integration of BCI with virtual reality (VR) applications. By combining BCI with VR technology, users can immerse themselves in virtual environments and interact with them using only their thoughts. This has significant implications for industries such as gaming and entertainment, where BCI-powered VR experiences can provide a whole new level of engagement and realism for users.

BCI technology is also making waves in the fields of robotics and prosthetics, where it is being used to control robotic limbs and assistive devices with unprecedented precision. By directly connecting the brain to these devices, individuals with disabilities can regain mobility and independence, opening up new possibilities for them in their daily lives. This integration of BCI with robotics holds great promise for the future of healthcare and rehabilitation.

In conclusion, the future of BCI in AI is full of exciting possibilities and potential implications across various industries. From neurofeedback and VR applications to robotics and prosthetics, BCI technology is poised to revolutionize how we interact with machines and AI systems. As we continue to explore the potential of BCI in AI, it is crucial to consider the ethical and privacy concerns that come with this technology, ensuring that it is used responsibly and for the benefit of all.